Jesse Johnson

Testimony of the Sonnets as to the

Authorship of the Shakespearean Plays and Poems

Jesse Johnson

Testimony of the Sonnets as to the
Authorship of the Shakespearean Plays and Poems

ISBN/EAN: 9783337063610

Printed in Europe, USA, Canada, Australia, Japan

Cover: Foto ©Thomas Meinert / pixelio.de

More available books at **www.hansebooks.com**

Testimony of the Sonnets as to the Authorship of the Shakespearean Plays and Poems

By Jesse Johnson

G. P. PUTNAM'S SONS

NEW YORK AND LONDON

The Knickerbocker Press

1899

The Knickerbocker Press, New York

DEDICATED TO
ALBERT E. LAMB
PARTNER AND FRIEND FOR TWENTY YEARS
OF THE ROYAL LINE OF LOYAL GENTLEMEN

CONTENTS

Contents

CHAPTER V

CHAPTER VI

INTRODUCTORY

THE Shakespearean Sonnets are not a single
or connected work like an ordinary play
or poem. Their composition apparently ex-
tended over a considerable time, which may
be fairly estimated as not less than four years.
Read literally they seem to portray thoughts,
modes or experiences fairly assignable to such
a period. Though variable and sometimes
light and airy in their movement, the greater
portion appear to reveal deep and intense
emotion, the welling and tumultous floods of
the inner life of their great author. And their
difficulty or mystery is, that they indicate
circumstances, surroundings, experiences and
regrets that we almost instinctively apprehend
could not have been those of William Shakespeare at the time they were written, when he
must have been in the strength of early manhood, in the warmth and glow of recent and
extraordinary advancement and success.

I

it is this difficulty that apparently has caused many to believe that their literal meaning cannot be accepted, and that we must give to them, or to many of them, a secondary meaning, founded on affectations or conceits relating to different topics or persons, or that at least we should not allow that in them the poet is speaking of himself. Others, like Grant White, simply allow and state the difficulty and leave it without any suggestion of solution.

Before conceding, however, that the splendid poetry contained in the Sonnets must be sundered or broken, or the apparent reality of its message doubted or denied, or that its message is mysterious or inexplicable—we should carefully inquire whether there is not some view or theory which will avoid the difficulties which have so baffled inquiry.

I believe that there is such a view or theory, and that view is—that the Sonnets were not written by Shakespeare, but were written to him as the patron or friend of the poet; that while Shakespeare may have been the author of some plays produced in his name at the theatre where he acted, or while he may have had a part in conceiving or framing the greater plays so produced, there was another, a great poet, whose dreamy and transforming genius wrought in and for them that which is imperishable, and so wrought although he was to have no part in their fame and perhaps but a small financial recompense; and that it is the loves, griefs, fears, forebodings and sorrows of the student and recluse, thus circumstanced and confined, that the Sonnets portray.

Considering that the Sonnets were so written, there is no need of any other than a literal and natural reading or interpretation. Commencing in expressions of gratulation and implied flattery, as they proceed, they appear to have been written as the incidents, fears and griefs which they indicate from time to time came; and it may well be that they were written not for publication, but as vents or expressions of a surcharged heart. With such a view of the situation of the poet and of his patron, we may not only understand much that otherwise is inexplicable, but we may understand why so much and such resplendent poetry is lavished on incidents so bare, meagre, and commonplace, and why they present both poet and patron with frailties and faults naked and repellant; and we can the better palliate and forgive the weakness and subjection which the Sonnets indicate on the part of their author. With such a reading the Sonnets become a chronicle of the modes and feelings of their author, resembling in this respect the *In Memoriam* of Tennyson; and their poetry becomes deeper and better, often equalling, if not surpassing in pathos and intensity anything in the greater Shakespearean plays.

Such is the result or conclusion to which the discussion which follows is intended to lead. I shall not, however, ask the reader to accept any such conclusion or result merely because it removes difficulties or because it makes or rather leaves the poetry better; but I shall present—that the Sonnets contain direct testimony, testimony not leading to surmise or conjecture, but testimony which would authorize a judgment in a court of law, that the Sonnets were not written by Shakespeare, and that they very strongly indicate that Shakespeare was the friend or patron to whom so many of them are addressed.

How such a conclusion from such testimony may be affected by arguments drawn from other sources I shall not discuss, contenting myself if into the main and larger controversy I have succeeded in introducing the effect and teaching of this, certainly, very valuable and important testimony.

TESTIMONY OF THE SONNETS AS TO THE AUTHORSHIP OF THE SHAKESPEAREAN PLAYS AND POEMS

CHAPTER I

OF THE CHARACTER OF THE SONNETS AND THEIR RELATION TO THE OTHER WORKS OF THE SAME AUTHOR

IN these pages I propose an examination and study of the Shakespearean Sonnets, for the purpose of ascertaining what information may be derived from them as to the authorship of the Shakespearean plays and poems. I am aware that any question or discussion as to their authorship is regarded with objection or impatience by very many. But to those not friendly to any such inquiry I would say, let us at least proceed so far as to learn precisely what the author of these great dramas says of himself and of his work in the only production in which he in any manner refers to or speaks of himself. Certainly an inquiry confined to such limits is appropriate, at least is not disloyal. And if we study the characters of Hamlet, Juliet or Rosalind, do we not owe it to the poet whose embodiments or creations they are, that we should study his character in the only one of his works in which his own surroundings and attachments, loves and fears, griefs and forebodings, appear to be at all indicated?

From the Homeric poems, Mr. Gladstone undertook to gather what they indicate as to the religion, morals and customs of the time; of the birthplace of the poet, and of the ethnology and migrations of the Hellenic peoples. Those poems were not written for any such purpose; they were for a people who, in the main, on all those subjects knew or believed as did their author. And it is both curious and instructive to note how much information as to that distant period Mr. Gladstone was able to gather from the circumstances, incidents, and implications of the Homeric poetry. The value of such deductions no one can question.

We may reject as myths the Trojan War or the wanderings or personality of Ulysses, but from these poems we certainly learn much of the method of warfare, navigation, agriculture, and of the social customs of those times.

So reading these Sonnets, we may perhaps not believe that the grief or love of the poet or the beauty of his friend was quite as great as the poetry indicates. But we may fairly take as correct what he says of his friend or of himself, as to their relations and companionship, the incidents and descriptions, which were but the framework on which he wove his poetic wreaths of affection, compliment, or regret.

But before entering on this inquiry, it is quite relevant to ascertain what relation these Sonnets bear to the Shakespearean plays and poems. The works of Shakespeare, as published, contain thirty - seven separate plays. Most of them are of the highest order, and rank with the most consummate products of poetic genius. But criticism seems to have established, and critics seem to agree, that in the works accredited to him are plays of a lower order, which certainly are not from the same author as the remainder, and especially the greater plays. In this widely different and lower class, criticism seems to be agreed in placing the greater portion of *Pericles*, *Titus Adronicus*, *Timon of Athens*, two parts of *Henry VI.*, and *Henry VIII.*[1] In addition to those, there are at least ten plays not now published as Shakespeare's, that are conceded to be of a lower order and by a different author, but which, apart from internal evidence, can be almost as certainly shown to be his work as many of the greater of the recognized Shakespearean plays. In the same high class of poetry as the greater of these dramas are the Sonnets; and they are unmistakably, and I think concededly, the work of the author of those greater plays.

It is of our poet, as the author of these greater dramas as well as of the Sonnets, that we would seek to learn in the study of the Sonnets. It is only in the Sonnets that the poet speaks in the first person, or allows us any suggestion of himself. His dramas reveal to us the characters he has imagined and desires to

---

[1] Brandes's *William Shakespeare, a Critical Study.* Temple edition of Shakespeare, introduction to plays above named.

portray; but they reveal nothing of the author. His two great poems are dramatic in substance and equally fail to give us any hint of their creator; but in the Sonnets his own is the character whose thoughts and emotions are stated. There we come nearest to him; and there it would seem that we should be able to learn very much of him. Perhaps we shall find that they do not present him at his best; it may be that they were intended only for the eye of the friend or patron to whom they are addressed. Perhaps they reveal the raveled sleeve, the anxieties of a straitened life and of narrow means. Certainly, while they reveal the wonderful fertility, resource, and fancy of the poet, they do not indicate that in outward semblance, surroundings or history their author was either fortunate or happy; and as we read them, sometimes we may feel that we are entering the poet's heart-home unbidden and unannounced. But if we have come there when it is all unswept and ungarnished, may we not the more certainly rely on what it indicates?

Before entering on the study of the Sonnets

we may inquire what, if anything, there is, distinctive of our great poet, the recognition of which may aid us in their interpretation.

Taine says that " the *creative* power is the poet's greatest gift, and communicates an extraordinary significance to his words "; and further, that " he had the prodigious faculty of seeing in a twinkling of an eye a complete character." [1]

The poet does not bring those characters to us by description, but he causes them to speak in words so true and apposite to the character he conceives that we seem to know the individuals from what they say and not from what the poet wrote or said. But the poet goes much farther, and in all his works presents surroundings and accessories, impalpable but certain, which fit the characters and their moods and actions. The picture of morning in *Venus and Adonis* is apposite to the rich, sensuous and brilliant colorings of the queen of love; the reference in *Romeo and Juliet* to the song of the nightingale " on yond' pomegranate tree " is but an incident to the soft, warm and love-

[1] Taine's *English Literature*, pp. 83, 84.

inviting night; Rosalind moves and talks to
the quickstep of the forest; in *Macbeth* the
incantation of the witches is but the outward
expression of an overmastering fate, whose
presence is felt throughout the play.   Let us
then, in studying the Sonnets, consider that
they are from the same great master as the
dramas.   And we shall be thus prepared,
where the meaning seems plain and obvious,
to believe that the writer meant what he said,
and to reject any interpretation which implies
that when he came to speak of himself he said
what he did not mean, or filled the picture with
descriptions, situations or emotions, incongruous or inappropriate.   And if in so reading
they seem clear and connected, fanciful and
far-drawn interpretations will not be adopted.
We should not distort or modify their meaning
in order to infer that they are imitations of
Petrarch, or that the genius of the poet, cribbed
and confined by the fashion of the time, forgot
to soar, and limped and waddled in the foot-
steps of the inconspicuous sonneteers of the
Elizabethan era.

I would illustrate my meaning.   Sonnet

CXXVI. is sometimes said to be an invocation
to Cupid.[1] That seems to me to destroy all its
grace and beauty. The first two lines of the
Sonnet,

> O thou, my lovely boy, who in thy power
> Dost hold Time's fickle glass, his sickle, hour—

are quite appropriate, if addressed to the god
of love. But the lines succeeding are quite
the reverse. In effect they say that you have
not grown old because Nature, idealized as an
active personality, has temporarily vanquished
Time, but will soon obtain the full audit. If
the Sonnet is addressed to the god of love it
reduces him to the limitations of mortality; if
it is addressed to his friend, it indicates that,
though but for a little while, Nature has lifted
him to an attribute of immortality. The latter
interpretation makes the poet enlarge and glo-
rify his subject; the former makes him belittle
it, and bring the god of love to the audit of age
and the ravage of wrinkles. This is the last
sonnet of the first series; with the next begins

[1] Lee's *Life of Shakespeare*, p. 27. The Sonnet is printed
in full at p. 28.

the series relating to his mistress. Reading it literally, considering it as addressed to his friend, it is sparkling and poetic, a final word, loving, admonitory, in perfect line and keeping with the central thought of all that came before. From this Sonnet, interpreted as I indicate, I shall try to find assistance in this study. But if it is a mere poetical ascription to Cupid, it, of course, tells us nothing except that its author was a poet.

I should not, however, leave this subject without stating that the fanciful interpretation of these Sonnets does not seem to be favored by more recent authors. I find no indication of such an interpretation in Taine's *English Literature*, or in Grant White's edition of Shakespeare. Professor Edward Dowden, universally recognized as a fair and competent critic, says: " The natural sense, I am convinced, is the true one." [1] Hallam says: " No one can doubt that they express not only real but intense emotions of the heart." [2] Professor Tyler, in a work relating to the

---

[1] Dowden, *Shakespeare: His Mind and Art*, pp. 102, 103.
[2] Hallam's *Literature of Europe*, Vol. II., Chap. V.

Sonnets, says: " The impress of reality is stamped on these Sonnets with unmistakable clearness." [1] Mr. Lee, while regarding some of these as mere fancies, obviously finds that many of them treated of facts.[2] Mr. Dowden, in a work devoted to the Sonnets, states very fully the views which have been expressed by different authors in relation to them. His quotations occupy sixty pages and, I think, clearly show that the weight of authority is decidedly in favor of allowing them their natural or primary meaning.

There are one hundred and fifty-four of these Sonnets. The last two are different in theme and effect from those which go before, and may perhaps not improperly be considered as mere exercises in poetizing. They have no connection with the others, and I would have no contention with those who regard them as suggested by Petrarch, or as complaisant imitations of the vogue or fashion of that time. Those two Sonnets I leave out of this discussion, and would have what may be here said,

---

[1] Tyler, *Shakespeare's Sonnets*, p. 10.
[2] Lee's *Life of Shakespeare*, pp. 97, 125, 126.

understood as applying only to the one hundred and fifty-two remaining.

These one hundred and fifty-two Sonnets I will now insist have a common theme. Most of them may be placed in groups which seem to be connected and somewhat interdependent. Those groups may perhaps, in some cases, be placed in different orders, without seriously affecting the whole. To that extent they are disconnected. But in whatever order those groups are placed, through them runs the same theme—the relations of the poet to his friend or patron, and to his mistress, the mistress of his carnal love, who is introduced only because the poet fears that she has transferred her affections or favors to his friend, wounding and wronging him in his love or desire for each.

It is easy to pick out many Sonnets which may be read as disconnected and independent poetry. But very many more verses could be selected from *In Memoriam* that can be read independently of the remainder of that poem. And there are none of the Sonnets, however they may read standing alone, that do not fit the mode and movement of those with which they stand connected. There is, I submit, no more reason for sundering Sonnets of that class from the others, than there is for taking the soliloquy of Hamlet from the play that bears his name.

This statement of the theme and the connected character of the Sonnets is not essential to the views I shall present. Nevertheless, if it is accepted, if we are able to agree that they all are relevant and apposite to a common theme, it strengthens the proposition that we should seek for them a literal meaning and should reject any construction which would make any of their description or movement incongruous to any other part. Of course we shall expect to find in them the enlargement or exaggeration of poetic license. But so doing we must recall the characteristics of their great author, who with all exaggeration preserves harmony and symmetry of parts, and harmony and correspondence in all settings and surroundings. With such views of what is fair and helpful in interpretation, I propose to proceed to a closer view of the first one hundred and fifty-two of what are known as the Sonnets of Shakespeare.

CHAPTER II

OF THE AGE OF THE WRITER OF THE SONNETS

ADOPTING the views which fix the later period as the date of the Sonnets, it seems practically certain that they were written as early as 1598,—though some of them may have been written as late as 1601,—and that a great portion were probably written as early as 1594.[1] Shakespeare was born in 1564. Consequently they appear to have been written when he was about thirty or thirty-four, certainly not over thirty-seven years of age.

It will be the main purpose of this chapter to call attention to portions of the Sonnets which seem to indicate that they were written by a man well past middle age,—perhaps fifty or sixty years old, and certainly not under forty years of age.

[1] Lee's *Life of Shakespeare*, p. 87 ; Preface to Sonnets, Temple Edition.

But before proceeding to the inquiry as to the age of the writer, I invite attention to what they indicate as to the age of the patron or friend to whom the first one hundred and twenty-six seem to have been written. In poetry as in perspective, there is much that is relative, and in the Sonnets the age of the writer and that of his friend are so often contrasted, that if with reasonable certainty, and within reasonable limits, we are able to state the age of his friend, we shall be well advanced toward fixing the age of the writer.

The first seventeen of these Sonnets are important in this connection. They have a common theme: it is that his friend is so fair, so incomparable, that he owes it to the world, to the poet, whose words of praise otherwise will not be believed, that he shall marry and beget a son. The whole argument clearly implies that the writer deems such admonition necessary, because his friend has passed the age when marriage is most frequent, and is verging toward the period of life when marriage is less probable. His friend appears to the writer as making a famine where abun-

dance lies; he tells him that he beguiles the
world, unblesses some mother; that he is his
mother's glass and calls back the April of her
prime; asks him why he abuses the bounteous
largess given him to give; calls him a profitless
usurer; tells him that the hours that have
made him fair will unfair him; that he should
not let winter's rugged hand deface ere he has
begotten a child, though it were a greater hap-
piness should he beget ten. He asks if his
failure to marry is because he might wet a
widow's eye, and then in successive Sonnets
cries shame on his friend for being so improvi-
dent. He tells him that when he shall wane,
change toward age, he should have a child to
perpetuate his youth; and the thought again
brings to the poet the vision of winter, summer's green borne on winter's bier, and he
urges him that he should prepare against his
coming end, by transmitting his semblance to
another; that he should not let so fair a house
fall to decay, but should uphold it against the
stormy blasts of winter by begetting a son;
seeing in his friend so much of beauty, he prog-
nosticates that his friend's end is beauty's

doom and date. Noting that nothing in nature
can hold its perfection long, he sees his friend,
most rich in youth, but Time debating with
decay, striving to change his day to night, and
urges him to make war upon the tyrant Time
by wedding a maiden who shall bear him living
flowers more like him than any painted coun-
terfeit. He tells him that could he adequately
portray his beauty, the world would make him
a liar, and then closes this theme by saying:

> But were some child of yours alive that time,
> You should live twice in it, and in my rhyme.

Any impression as to the age of the poet's
friend which this brief synopsis of the first
seventeen Sonnets conveys, I think will be increased by reading the Sonnets themselves.
I have refrained from stating any portions of
Sonnets II. and VII., desiring to present to
the reader their exact words. Sonnet VII.
reads as follows:

> Lo! in the orient when the gracious light
> Lifts up his burning head, each under eye
> Doth homage to his new-appearing sight,
> Serving with looks his sacred majesty;

And having *climb'd the steep-up heavenly hill,*
Resembling strong youth in his middle age,
Yet mortal looks adore his beauty still,
Attending on his golden pilgrimage;
But when from highmost pitch, with weary car,
Like feeble age, he reeleth from the day,
The eyes, 'fore duteous, now converted are
From his low tract, and look another way:
  So thou, thyself out-going in thy noon,
  Unlook'd on diest, unless thou get a son.

The poet sees his friend, as is the sun after it
has climbed the morning steep and is journey-
ing on the level heaven toward the zenith.
Certainly that must indicate that his friend
was advanced toward the middle arch of life.

Sonnet II. reads as follows:

When *forty* winters shall besiege thy brow
And dig deep trenches in thy beauty's field,
Thy youth's proud livery, so gazed on now,
Will be a tatter'd weed, of small worth held:
Then, being ask'd where all thy beauty lies,
Where all the treasure of thy lusty days,
To say, within thine own deep-sunken eyes,
Were an all-eating shame, and thriftless praise.

  .   .   .   .   .   .

  This were to be new made when thou art old,
  And see thy blood warm when thou feel'st it cold.

These lines indicate that his friend had not yet reached forty years. And equally do they indicate that in the mind of the poet the fortieth year was not in the ascending scale of life, but was at, or perhaps beyond, the " highmost pitch " toward which, in the seventh Sonnet, he described his friend as approaching.[1]

Taking these seventeen Sonnets together, reading and re-reading them, can we suppose that they were composed by the great delineator, of or toward a person under or much below thirty? They imply that the person addressed was not so far below middle life that a statement of the decadence that would come after his fortieth year presented a remote or far-off picture. Besides, if his friend was below thirty years, while it might be well to urge him to marry, hardly would the poet have used language implying that his marrying days were

---

[1] In a note to page 30 is the poet's familiar expression or statement of the Seven Ages of man. It clearly places the decade from forty to fifty as past the middle arch of life, and next to the age of the slippered pantaloon and shrunk shank ; from thirty to forty he describes as the age of the soldier, and from twenty to thirty that of the lover.

waning. To put it roughly, there would not be so much of the now-or-never thought running through the ornate verse in which the poet voices his appeal.

As we read these seventeen Sonnets, we may perhaps suspect that the desire that his friend shall marry is so strongly stated and presented, because it is a theme around which the poet can appropriately weave so much of compliment and expressions of admiration and affection. But if that be so, must we not still believe that the great dramatist could not have addressed them to his friend, unless in substance and in all their more delicate shades of meaning and of coloring they were appropriate to him ?

We may now pass from this first group to other Sonnets which convey similar and, I submit, unmistakable intimations as to the age of the poet's friend or patron.

Sonnet C., especially when read with the one preceding, clearly indicates that it was written as a greeting or salutation after absence, and on the poet's return to his friend. In it he says:

Rise, resty Muse, my love's sweet face survey,—
If Time have any wrinkle graven there ;
If any, be a satire to decay,
And make *Time's spoils* despised everywhere.
    Give my love fame faster *than Time wastes life ;*
    So thou prevent'st his scythe and crooked knife.

    Closely following, in Sonnet CIV., the poet says:

To me, fair friend, *you never can be old,*
For as you were when first your eye I eyed,
Such seems your beauty still. Three winters cold,[1]

    .   .   .   .   .   .

In process of the seasons have I seen,

    .   .   .   .   .   .

Since first I saw you fresh, which yet are green.
Ah! yet doth beauty, like a dial-hand,
Steal from his figure, and no pace perceived;
So your sweet hue, which methinks still doth stand,
Hath motion, and mine eye may be deceived [2]:

[1] It is generally considered that the first of the Shakespearean plays was produced in 1591. If they were written by an unknown poet and brought out or published by Shakespeare, the time between their first joint venture and the earlier date assumed for these Sonnets, would be *three years.*

[2] Th phrase " mine eye may be deceived," may also throw some light of another subject discussed in this chapter,—the age of the poet. Such an expression would seem much more natural to a person above, than to a person below, forty years of age.

For fear of which, hear this, thou age unbred;
Ere you were born was beauty's summer dead.

The thought is: your beauty may be passing; it may be that my eye that sees it not,
is deceived. We should carefully note the
words, " Three winters cold," " Since first I
saw you fresh, which *yet* are green." Though
they present no clear or sharp indication as to
the age of his friend, yet I think that of them
this may be fairly said: the word " green " is
used as opposed to ripe or matured, and his
friend's age is such that three years seem to
the poet to have carried him a step toward
maturity. And so reading these words, they
harmonize with the expression of the poet's
fear that his great love for his friend may have
prevented him from seeing his beauty

like a dial hand,
Steal from his figure.

In Sonnet LXX. the poet says of his friend :

And thou present'st a pure unstained *prime*.
Thou hast pass'd by *the ambush of young days*,
Either not assail'd, or victor being charged.

In Sonnet LXXVII. the poet says:

The wrinkles which thy glass will truly show
Of mouthed graves will give thee memory;
Thou by thy dial's shady stealth mayst know
Time's thievish progress to eternity.

Sonnet CXXVI. is as follows:

O thou, my lovely boy, who in thy power
Dost *hold Time's fickle glass, his sickle, hour ;*
Who hast by waning grown, and therein show'st
Thy *lovers withering as thy sweet self grow'st ;*
If Nature, sovereign mistress over wrack,
As thou goest onwards, *still* will pluck thee back,
She keeps thee to this purpose, that her skill
May *time disgrace* and wretched *minutes* kill.
Yet fear her, O thou minion of her pleasure!
She may *detain*, but not *still* keep, her treasure:
   Her audit, though delay'd, answer'd must be,
   And her quietus is to render thee.

This is the last Sonnet which the poet addresses to his friend. Except the last two, all that follow are of his mistress, and are of the same theme as Sonnets XL., XLI., and XLII., and, we may fairly infer, are of the same date. If so, Sonnet CXXVI. is practically the very latest of the entire series, and we may deem it a leave-taking, perhaps not of his friend, but of the labor that had so long moved him.

Perhaps for that reason its words should be deemed more significant, and it should be read and considered more carefully.' All its thoughts seem responsive to the central suggestion that his friend appears much younger than he is. To the poet he seems still a boy because he has so held the youth and freshness of boyhood that it is not inappropriate to say that he holds in his power the glass of Time; Nature has plucked him back to show her triumph over Time, but she cannot continue to do so, but will require of him full audit for all his years.

For what age do such expressions seem natural as words of compliment; and when first would it have pleased us to be told that we looked younger than we were, and to one that loved us, still seemed but as a boy? Hardly much before thirty; till then we took but little account of years and would have preferred to be told that we seemed manlier rather than younger than we were. But on this let us further consult our poet. He tells us that at

<hr />

[1] See discussion of claim that this Sonnet was addressed to Cupid, pages 14, 15.

ten begins the age of the whining school-boy;
at twenty of the lover, sighing like a furnace,
and that of the soldier, a vocation of manhood,
at thirty.[1] To me it seems very clear that the

[1] *As You Like It*, Act II., Sc. VII. :

" All the world 's a stage,
And all the men and women merely players :
They have their exits and their entrances ;
And one man in his time plays many parts,
His acts being seven ages.   At first the infant,
Mewling and puking in the nurse's arms.
Then the whining school-boy, with his satchel
And shining morning face, creeping like snail
Unwillingly to school.   And then the lover,
Sighing like furnace, with a woeful ballad
Made to his mistress' eyebrow.   Then a soldier,
Full of strange oaths, and bearded like the pard,
Jealous in honour, sudden and quick in quarrel,
Seeking the bubble reputation
Even in the cannon's mouth.   And then the justice,
In fair round belly with good capon lined,
With eyes severe and beard of formal cut,
Full of wise saws and modern instances ;
And so he plays his part.   The sixth age shifts
Into the lean and slipper'd pantaloon,
With spectacles on nose and pouch on side,
His youthful hose, well saved, a world too wide
For his shrunk shank ; and his big manly voice,
Turning again toward childish treble, pipes
And whistles in his sound.   Last scene of all,
That ends this strange eventful history,
Is second childishness and mere oblivion,
Sans teeth, sans eyes, sans taste, sans every thing."

rich poetic fancy of this Sonnet would be greatly lessened by assuming it to be addressed to a person below twenty-five years of age, and if it came, as may hereafter appear, from a person of fifty years or over, its caressing compliments and admonition would seem quite appropriate for one who had reached the fourth age of life. The indication of the last four Sonnets, to which I have referred, I submit, is in entire accord with that of the first group of seventeen.

I would not, however, leave this branch of the discussion without indicating what I deem is the fair inference or result from it. I do not claim that the age of the poet's friend can be certainly stated from anything contained in the Sonnets. It seems to me, however, that it mars the poetry and makes its notes seem inappropriate and discordant, to suppose that the poet had in mind a person below twenty-five years of age. To do so would make some, at least, of his terms of description inapt, subtract from the sparkle and force of his compliments, and cause his words of loving admonition and advice to appear ill-timed and inappropriate. Certainly the Sonnets indicate that his friend was on the morning side of life and below forty; and perhaps ten or twelve years below would best fit the verse. It may be, probably it is the fact, that a number of years, from four to seven, elapsed between the earliest and the latest of these Sonnets; and that may explain why we are not able to find any more specific indications as to the age of his friend.

There are also Sonnets from which it has been inferred that the poet's friend was much younger than thirty, and possibly or probably below twenty years of age. A careful examination of these Sonnets will, however, I think very clearly indicate that no such inference can be fairly drawn.

In Sonnet LIV. the poet says:

And so of you, beauteous and lovely youth,
When that shall fade, my verse distills your truth.

In Sonnet XCVI. he says:

Some say, thy fault is youth, some wantonness;
Some say, thy grace is youth and gentle sport;

Similar expressions appear in Sonnets II.,
XV., XXXIII., and XLI.

In Sonnet CXIV. he says:

Such cherubins as your sweet self resemble.

Sonnet CXXVI., containing the appellation,
" my lovely boy," has been already quoted.[1]

In Sonnet CVIII. he says:

What 's in the brain, that ink may character,
Which hath not figured to thee my true spirit?
What 's new to speak, what new to register,
That may express my love, or thy dear merit?
Nothing, *sweet boy ;* but yet, like prayers divine,
I must each day say o'er the very same;
Counting no old thing old, thou mine, I thine,
Even as when first I hallowed thy fair name.
So that eternal love in love's fresh case
Weighs not the dust and injury of age,
Nor gives to necessary wrinkles place,
But makes antiquity for aye his page ;
   Finding the *first* conceit of love there bred,
   Where *time* and *outward form* would show it
     dead.

Hardly could any argument for extreme
youth be made from any of these lines, except
as based on the term " boy." The term

[1] Page 28, *supra.*

" youth " obviously has a broader significance, and by no strained construction, especially if coming from a man of advanced
years, may be applied to persons on the morning side of life without any precise or clear
reference to, or indication of, their age. We
should therefore turn to the lines containing
the appellation " boy " for whatever of force
there is in the claim for the extreme youth of
the poet's friend. Doing so, the context in
each case clearly indicates that no such inference can be fairly drawn. In the Sonnet last
quoted (CVIII.), the poet, saying that there is
nothing new to register of his love for his
friend, and that he counts nothing old that is
so used, then says that his eternal love

> Weighs not the dust and injury of age,
> Nor gives to necessary wrinkles place.

Hardly could he have said plainer that his
loving appellation, " sweet boy," is made because he can allow neither his friend, nor his
love for him, nor his own frequent recurring
expressions of it, to grow old; the last two
lines of the Sonnet, referring to the indications

of time and outward form, seem to be a continuance and enlargement of the same thought.

So interpreting his verse it is fresh, sparkling, and complimentary; but deeming that the person addressed was sixteen or twenty years old, indeed a mere boy, at least half of the portion of the Sonnet following the term " sweet boy " is inappropriate and useless. This Sonnet, I think, might be cited as indicating that, except to the eye of love, that is in sober fact, the poet's friend was no longer a boy.

Sonnet CXXVI., is quoted at page 28, and discussed, and presented as clearly stating that his friend was termed a boy only because, as to him, Time had been hindered and delayed.

There is, however, a further consideration which I think should effectually dispose of any doubts that may remain on account of the use of the words " youth " or " boy." In the succeeding portions of this chapter I shall quote Sonnets indicating, indeed saying, that the poet was on the sunset side of life— probably fifty years of age or older, and so at least twenty years older than is indicated of his friend, except in the Sonnets now being considered. If the poet was fifty years of age or more, the terms here discussed are amply and fully satisfied without ascribing to them any definite indication as to the age of the person addressed. To a person of the age of fifty or sixty years, addressing a person young enough to be his son, especially if of a fair and youthful appearance, the expressions " boy " or " youth " come quite naturally and have no necessary significance beyond indicating the *relative* age of the person so addressed.[1] And especially is this so when the

[1] In Lee's *Life of Shakespeare*, p. 143, appear some statements so relevant to this discussion that I cannot forbear quoting them :

" Octavius Cæsar at thirty-two is described by Mark Antony after the battle of Actium as the 'boy Cæsar' who ' wears the rose of youth' (*Antony and Cleopatra*, III., ii., 17 *seq.*). Spenser in his *Astrophel* apostrophizes Sir Philip Sidney on his death near the close of his thirty-second year as ' oh wretched boy' (l. 133) and 'luckless boy' (l. 142)."

I was at a public dinner given some years ago, at which General Henry W. Slocum and Colonel Fred Grant were both speakers. In his remarks, the General, having stated that his friend the Colonel spoke to him about being a candidate for an office, continued, " I said to him, ' Why, Fred, you are a mere boy,' and his answer to me was, ' Why, General, I am as old as my father was when he took Vicksburg.'" General Grant was then forty years old.

words are used in expressions of affection and of familiar or caressing endearment.

With such aid as may be had from considering the age of his friend, we come to the more important inquiry: WHAT WAS THE AGE OF THE AUTHOR OF THESE SONNETS, — WHAT WAS THE AGE OF THE POET OF THE SHAKESPEAREAN PLAYS? I shall present that which indicates that HE WAS PROBABLY FIFTY, PERHAPS SIXTY, CERTAINLY MORE THAN FORTY YEARS OF AGE at the time he wrote the Sonnets.

But if our great poet was forty,—probably if he was thirty-five years of age, when these Sonnets were composed,—he was born before 1564, before the birth date of William Shakespeare.

The poet clearly indicates that he is older than his friend. In Sonnet XXII. he says:

My glass shall not persuade me I am old,
So long as *youth and thou* are of one date;
But when in thee time's furrows I behold,
Then look I death my days should expiate.
For all that beauty that doth cover thee
Is but the seemly raiment of my heart,

Which in thy breast doth live, as thine in me:
How can I then be *elder* than thou art ?

In Sonnet LXXIII. he speaks directly of
his own age or period of life, as follows:

That *time of year* thou mayst in me behold
When yellow leaves, or none, or few, do hang
Upon those boughs which shake against the cold,
Bare ruin'd choirs, where late the sweet birds
    sang.
In *me* thou seest the *twilight* of such day
As *after sunset* fadeth in the west;
Which by and by black night doth take away,
Death's second self, that seals up all in rest.
In me *thou see'st the glowing of such fire,*
That on the ashes of his youth doth lie,
As the death-bed whereon it must expire,
Consumed with that which it was nourish'd by.
    This thou perceivest, which makes thy love more
        strong,
    To *love that well which thou must leave ere long.*

The latter part of Sonnet LXII. and Sonnet
LXIII. are as follows:

But when my glass shows me myself indeed,
Beated and chopp'd with tann'd antiquity,
Mine own self-love quite contrary I read;
Self so self-loving were iniquity.

'T is thee, myself, that for myself I praise,
Painting *my age with* beauty of thy days.

Against my love shall be, *as I am now*,
With Time's injurious hand crush'd and o'erworn;
When hours have drain'd his blood and fill'd his brow
With lines and wrinkles ; when his youthful morn
Hath travell'd on to *age's steepy night*,
And all those beauties whereof now he 's king
Are vanishing or vanish'd out of sight,
Stealing away the treasure of his spring;
For such a time do I now fortify
Against confounding age's cruel knife,
That he shall never cut from memory
My sweet love's beauty, though my lover's life:
   His beauty shall in these black lines be seen,
   And they shall live, and he in them still green.

It should be noted that the poet is picturing
no morning cloud or storm or eclipse; but his
grief is that he has had his morning and his
noon and that he is now at " age's steepy
night " *because his sun has travelled so far in
his life's course.* The Sonnet seems to be the
antithesis of Sonnet VII., quoted at page 22.
The metaphor is the same, comparing life to
the daily journey of the sun. In each, the
poet views the *steep* of the journey, the earlier

and the later hours of the day; and while he finds that his friend's age is represented by the sun passing from the "steep-up" hill to the zenith, with equal clearness and certainty he indicates that his age is represented by its last and declining course, that *he* has "travelled on to *age's steepy night*." As clearly as words can say, the poet states that he is on the sunset side of life and indicates that he is well advanced toward its close.

Sonnet CXXXVIII. is as follows:

When my love swears that she is made of truth,
I do believe her, *though I know she lies*,
That she might think me some untutor'd youth,
Unlearned in the world's false subtleties.
Thus *vainly* thinking that she thinks me young,
Although she knows my days are past the best,
Simply I credit her false-speaking tongue:
On both sides thus is simple truth suppress'd.
But wherefore says she not she is unjust?
And wherefore say not I that I am old?
O, love's best habit is in seeming trust,
And *age in love loves not to have years told:*
   Therefore I lie with her and she with me,
   And in our faults by lies we flatter'd be.

The poet is here speaking of his mistress, the

mistress of his carnal love, who had in act her bed-vow broke (Sonnet CLII.). Having stated that when she swears she is true he knows she lies, he adopts the conceit of asserting that he is not old, as an equivalent to her obvious falsehood in saying that she is not unjust. This is one of twenty-six Sonnets relating to his mistress and her desertion of him for his friend. In Sonnets XL., XLI., and XLII. he complains to his friend of the same wrong.

The fact that the poet found a subject for his verse in such an occurrence has been much commented on. Poetic fancy would hardly have chosen such a theme, and these Sonnets seem to be certainly based on an actual occurrence. And if so, certainly we may construe them very literally ; and read literally they certainly appear to be an old man's lament at having been superseded by a younger though much loved rival.

William Shakespeare was a prosperous, a very successful man. In twenty years he accumulated property which made him a rich man, — yielding a yearly income of $5000, equivalent to $25,000 dollars at the present

time.   He was an actor publicly accredited as
a man of amorous gallantries[1]; he married at
eighteen, apparently in haste, and less than
six months before the birth of a child.[2] We
know from legal records that he and his father
before him had frequent lawsuits.[3] While a
uniform tradition represents him as comely,
pleasing and attractive, equally does it represent him as a man of ready, aggressive and
caustic wit, and rebellious and bitter against
opposition.[4] The lines on the slab over his
grave are less supplicatory than mandatory
against the removal of his bones to the adjacent charnel-house.[5] His name, often written
with a hyphen, indicates that he came of English fighting stock.   When the Sonnets were
written he was in the full tide of success.   It
is not credible that such a man at thirty or
thirty-five, of buoyant and abounding life,
could have so bewailed the loss of a mistress.

Mr. Lee says that the Sonnets last quoted

[1] Post., pp. 68–70.
[2] Lee's *Shakespeare*, pp. 19–22.
[3] Post., pp. 66–68.
[4] Post., pp. 60–66.
[5] Post., p. 66.

admit of no literal interpretation.[1] In other
words, as I understand, he concedes that a literal interpretation is destructive of what he
assumes to be the fact as to the authorship of
the Shakespearean plays. By what right or
rule of construction does he refuse them their
literal reading ? They indicate no hidden or
double meaning, but seem direct though poetic
statements of conditions and resulting reflections and feelings. And more than that, though
appearing in separate groups, their indications
as to age all harmonize, and are not in conflict
with any other part or indication of the Sonnets. Mr. Lee urges that these Sonnets were
mere affectations, conceits common to the poets
of that day. That view will not bear investi-
gation. He cites passages from poets of that
time ascribing to themselves in youth the ills,
the miseries, the wrinkles, the white hairs of
age. But such is not the effect of what has
been here quoted. The poet says that it is *his
age* that oppresses him, and brings him its ills
and marks and ravages; and about as clearly
as poetic description is capable of, indicates

[1] Lee's *Shakespeare*, p. 85.

and says that he is on the sunset side of his
day of life. I cannot at this instant quote, but
I am impressed that in the plays of the great
poet, the instances are frequent where sorrow
or despair bring his youthful characters to picture their lot with the deprivations, the ills
or forebodings of age. But in no such passages is language used which is at all equivalent to that here quoted. Nowhere does he
present such a travesty as to allow Juliet to
describe herself in good straight terms that
would befit her grandmother; and there is
nothing that the much-lamenting Hamlet says
which would lead an actor to play the part
with the accessories of age and feebleness with
which they represent Polonius.

Having now called attention to these Sonnets which give direct indications as to the age
of the poet, I ask the reader to consider again
those which I have quoted in relation to the
age of his friend, and particularly Sonnets II.
and VII. (pp. 22 and 23). If those Sonnets
came from a poet of the age and infirmities
which a literal reading indicates, how forceful,
strong, and poetic is their appeal. But if it

is to be assumed that they were written by a
man of thirty or thirty-five, strong, vigorous,
aggressive, fortunate, and successful, the appeal seems out of harmony, and lacks that
delicate adaptation of speech to surroundings
which is characteristic of the author.

I would next call attention to portions of
these Sonnets which I do not present as of
themselves having any clearly determinate
weight as to the age of the poet, but which
do have great significance from their correspondence in tone and effect with what has
been already quoted. The poet repeatedly
falls into meditations or fancies which seem
more natural to a person on the descending
than on the ascending side of life.

In Sonnets XXX. and XXXI. he says:

When to the sessions of sweet silent thought
I summon up *remembrance of things past,*
I sigh the lack of many a thing I sought,
And with old woes *new wail my dear time's waste :*
Then can I drown an eye, unused to flow,
For *precious friends hid in death's dateless night,*
And weep afresh love's *long since* cancell'd woe,
And moan the expense of many a vanish'd sight:

Then can I grieve at grievances foregone,
And heavily from woe to woe tell o'er
The sad account of fore-bemoaned moan,
Which I new pay, as if not paid before.

   .   .   .   .

Thy bosom is endeared with *all hearts*,
Which I *by lacking have supposed dead ;*
And there reigns love, and all love's loving parts,
And all those *friends which I thought buried.*
How many *a holy and obsequious tear*
Hath dear, religious love stol'n from mine eye,
As *interest of the dead*, which now appear
But things removed that hidden in thee lie!
Thou art the grave *where buried love doth live,*
Hung with the *trophies of my lovers gone,*
Who all their parts of me to thee did give:
That due of many now is thine alone:

  In Sonnet LXXI. he says:

No longer *mourn for me when I am dead*
Than you shall hear the surly sullen bell
Give warning to the world *that I am fled*
From this vile world, with vilest worms to dwell:
Nay, if you read this line, remember not
The hand that writ it; for I love you so,
That I in your sweet thoughts would be forgot,
If thinking on me then should make you woe.

  In Sonnet CXXII. he says:

Thy gift, thy tables, are within my brain

   .   .   .   .

Beyond all date, even to eternity:
Or, at the least, *so long as brain and heart*
Have faculty by nature to subsist;
Till each to razed oblivion yield his part.

In Sonnet CXLVI. he says:

Poor soul, the centre of my sinful earth,
. . . . these rebel powers that thee array,
Why dost thou pine within and suffer dearth,
Painting thy outward walls so costly gay ?
Why so large cost, having *so short* a lease,
Dost thou upon thy fading mansion spend ?
Shall worms, inheritors of this excess,
Eat up thy charge ? is this thy body's end ?
Then, soul, live thou upon thy servant's loss,
And let that pine to aggravate thy store;
Buy terms divine in selling hours of dross;
Within be fed, without be rich no more:
So shalt thou feed on Death, that feeds on men,
And Death once dead, there 's no more dying
then.

In Sonnets LXVI. and LXXIV. appear
further similar meditations. Such thoughts
and meditations do not seem to be those of
the successful and prosperous man of thirty or
thirty-five.

The persuasive force of the Sonnets which
have been quoted or referred to in this chapter

is much increased by reading or considering
them together. To illustrate: four Sonnets
have been quoted containing direct statements by the poet that he was in the
afternoon of life. It needs no argument to
establish that this concurrence of statements
made in different groups of Sonnets and doubtless at different times has much more than
four times the persuasive force of one such
statement. And in like ratio do the other
Sonnets indicating the reflections and conditions of age, increase the weight of the statements in these four Sonnets. Taking them
all together they seem to present the statements, conditions, and reflections of a man
certainly past the noon of life,—past forty
years of age, and so older than was Shakespeare at the time of their composition.

If this conclusion is correct, it does not aid,
but about equally repels the claim that Bacon
was the author of the Sonnets, or of the plays
or poems produced by the same poet. Bacon
was born in 1561, and was therefore but three
years older than Shakespeare.

CHAPTER III

SONNETS LV. and LXXXI. are as follows:

Not marble, nor the gilded monuments
Of princes, shall outlive this powerful rhyme;
But *you* shall shine more bright in these contents
Than unswept stone, besmear'd with sluttish time.
When wasteful war shall statues overturn,
And broils root out the work of masonry,
Nor Mars his sword nor war's quick fire shall burn
The living record of *your memory*.
'Gainst death and all-oblivious enmity
Shall *you* pace forth; your praise shall still find room
Even in the eyes of all posterity
That wear this world out to the ending doom.
   So, till the judgment that yourself arise,
   You live in this, and dwell in lovers' eyes.

Or I shall live your epitaph to make,
Or you survive when I in earth am rotten;
From hence *your* memory death cannot take,
Although in *me* each part will be forgotten.
Your name from hence immortal life shall have,

49

Though I, once gone, *to all the world must die :*
The earth can yield *me* but a common grave,
When *you* entombed in men's eyes shall lie.
Your monument shall be *my gentle verse,*
Which eyes not yet created shall o'er-read;
And tongues to be *your* being shall rehearse,
When all the breathers of this world are dead;
  You still shall live—such virtue hath *my* pen—
  Where breath most breathes, even in the mouths
    of men.

In all the plays and poems of Shakespeare, including these Sonnets, there is no mention of any man or woman then living. The only mention of a person then living made by our poet, either in prose or verse, is in the dedication of the two poems to the Earl of Southampton. To Shakespeare, to Shakespeare alone, have the Shakespearean poems and plays been a monument; and for him have they done precisely that which the poet says his " gentle verse " was to do for his friend; and they have not done so in any degree for any other.

An anonymous writer in Chambers's *Edinburgh Journal*, in August, 1852, seems to have been one of the first to suggest the doubt as

to the authorship of the Shakespearean plays.
His suggestion was that their real author was
" some pale, wasted student . . . with
eyes of genius gleaming through despair "
who found in Shakespeare a purchaser, a publisher, a friend, and a patron. If that theory
is correct, the man that penned those Sonnets
sleeps, as he said he would, in an unrecorded
grave, while his publisher, friend and patron,
precisely as he also said, has a place in the
Pantheon of the immortals.

Very many of these Sonnets seem to be
evolved from, or kindred to, the thought so
sharply presented in Sonnets LV. and LXXXI.
I would refer the reader particularly to Sonnets
XXXVIII., XLIX., LXXI., LXXII., and
LXXXVIII. The last two lines of Sonnet
LXXI. are as follows:

Lest the *wise* world should look into your moan,
And mock you with me after I am gone.

The first lines of Sonnet LXXII. are as
follows:

O! lest the world should task you to recite
What merit lived in me, that you should love

After my death, dear love, forget me quite,
For you in me can nothing worthy prove;
Unless you would devise some virtuous lie,
To do more for me than mine own desert,
And hang more praise upon deceased I
Than *niggard* truth would *willingly* impart:

Many of these Sonnets, which otherwise
seem entirely inexplicable, and which have for
that reason been held to be imitations or
strange and unnatural conceits, become true
and genuine and much more poetic, if we conceive them to be written, not by the accredited
author of the Shakespearean dramas, but by the
unnamed and unknown student whose connection with them was carefully concealed.   I
suggest that the reader test this statement by
carefully reading the four Sonnets last mentioned.

The claim for a literal reading of Sonnet
LXXXI. is greatly strengthened by its context, by reading it with the group of Sonnets
of which it forms a part.   Sonnets LXXVII.
to XC. all more or less relate to another poet,
who, the author fears, has supplanted him in
the affection, or it may be, in the patronage of

his friend. That particularly appears in Sonnet LXXXVI.:

Was it the proud full sail of his great verse,
Bound for the prize of all too precious you,
That did my ripe thoughts in my brain inhearse,
Making their tomb the womb wherein they grew ?
Was it *his* spirit, by spirits taught to write
Above a mortal pitch, that struck me dead ?
No, neither he, nor his compeers by night
Giving him aid, my verse astonished.
He, nor that affable familiar ghost
Which nightly gulls him with intelligence,
As victors, of my silence cannot boast;
I was not sick of any fear from thence:
But when your countenance fill'd up his line,
Then lack'd I matter; that enfeebled mine.

That what is there stated as to another poet
refers to an actual transaction, and is to be
read literally, is recognized, I think, by all
critics; and many have thought that the description contained in the Sonnet quoted indicates Chapman, who translated the *Iliad* about
that time. It is in this group of Sonnets,
referring to another poet, that we find Sonnet
LXXXI. The thought of the entire group is

complaint, perhaps jealousy, of a rival poet; and running through them all are allusions or statements which seem to have been intended to strengthen the ties between him and his friend,—to hold him if he meditated going, and to bring him back if he had already strayed. It was obviously for that purpose that Sonnet LXXXI., one of the central Sonnets of that group, was written; and, considered as written for that purpose, how apt and true its language appears! The poet, asserting that his verse is immortal, says to his friend, the immortality it confers is yours; "your name from hence immortal life shall have," but I shall have no share in that fame; " in me each part will be forgotten," and " earth can yield me but a common grave." Though the Sonnet is in the highest degree poetic, as a bare statement of fact it is perfectly apt and appropriate to that which was the obvious purpose of this group of Sonnets.

It is sometimes claimed that the author of the Shakespearean plays was a lawyer. Certainly he was a logician and a rhetorician. The clash of minds and of speech appearing in *Julius*

Cæsar, in *Antony and Cleopatra*, in *Henry IV.*, and in many other plays, shows a most wonderful facility for stating a case, for presenting an argument. Let us then assume that the poet was simply stating his own case against a rival poet, presenting his own appeal,—and the verse at once has added dignity and passion, and we almost feel the poet's heart throb. Of course the final question—whether or not the two Sonnets printed at the head of this chapter were founded on the conditions and situations they state, and whether or not they express actual feelings and emotions—must be answered by each from a careful reading of the Sonnets themselves. To me, however, their message of sadness, loneliness, and implied appeal seems as clear and certain as the portrayal of agony in the marble of Laocoön.

That Sonnet LV., and perhaps in some degree Sonnet LXXXI., are moulded after verses of Ovid or Horace, is often mentioned. And it is mentioned as though that somehow detracted from their meaning or force. That fact seems to me rather to reinforce that meaning. The words of Ovid are translated as follows:

Now have I brought a work to an end which neither
    Jove's fierce wrath,
Nor sword nor fire nor fretting age with all the force
    it hath,
Are able to abolish quite.[1]

The Ode of Horace has been translated as follows:

A monument on stable base,
More strong than Brass, my Name shall grace;
Than Regal Pyramids more high
Which Storms and Years unnumber'd shall defy.

My nobler Part shall swiftly rise
Above this Earth, and claim the Skies.[2]

Agreeing that the poet had in mind the words of Ovid and of Horace and believed that his productions would outlast bronze or marble, we see that, so far following their thoughts, by a quick transition he says that not he, but his friend, is to have the immortality that his poetry will surely bring. While this comparison with the Latin poems may not much aid an interpretation that seemed clear and certain without it, at least its sudden rending from

---

[1] Ovid's *Metamorphoses*, xv., 871–9.
[2] Horace, Book III., Ode XXX.

their thought does not weaken, but strengthens
the effect of the statement that the writer was
to have no part in the immortality of his own
poetry.

It may be said that it is entirely improbable
that the author of the greater of the Shakespearean plays should have allowed their guer-
don of fame and immortality to pass to and
remain with another. But if we accept the
results of the later criticism, we must then
agree,—that there were at least three poets
who wrought in and for the Shakespearean
plays, that two of the three consented that
their work should go to the world as that of
another, and that at least one of the two was
a poet of distinctive excellence. At that time
the publication and sale of books was very
limited and the relative rights of publishers
and authors were such that the author had but
little or none of the pecuniary results. The
theatre was the most promising and hence the
most usual market for literary work, and it
seems certain that poets and authors sold
their literary productions to the managers of
theatres, retaining no title or interest in them.

However the poet of the Shakespearean plays
may have anticipated the verdict of posterity,
the plays bear most abundant evidence that
they were written to be acted, to entertain and
please, and to bring patrons and profit to the
theatres which were in the London of three
hundred years ago.

Boucicault was the publisher and accredited
author of one hundred and thirty plays. But
no one would deem it improbable that in them
is the work of another, or of many other
dramatists.

I submit that the argument from probabili-
ties is without force against the clear and
unambiguous statements of the Sonnets quoted
in this chapter.

CHAPTER IV

OF THE CHARACTER OF SHAKESPEARE AS
RELATED TO THE CHARACTER OF THE
AUTHOR OF THE SONNETS

THE Sonnets certainly reveal their author
in an attitude of appeal, more or less
open and direct, for the love or favor of his
friend. No fervor of compliment or protesta-
tion of affection allows him to forget or con-
ceal this purpose. When, as is indicated by
Sonnets LXXVII. to XC., he feared that his
friend was transferring his favor or patronage to
another poet, his anxiety became acute, and
in that group he compared not only his poetry,
but his flattery and commendation with that of
his rival. In Sonnets XXXII. to XXXVII.,
portraying his grief at his friend's unkindness,
he hastens to forgive; and, as already stated,
in Sonnets XL. to XLIII. and CXXVII. to
CLII., chiding his friend for having accepted
the love of his mistress, he crowns him with

poetic garlands of compliment and adulation.
Smitten on one cheek, not only does he turn
the other, but he bestows kisses and caresses
on the hand that gave the blow.

All we know of the character of Shakespeare
indicates that he was neither meek and complacent, nor quick and eager in forgiving; but
that his character in those aspects was quite
the reverse of the character of the author of
the Sonnets.

Mr. Lee states the effect or result of the
various traditions as to Shakespeare's poaching
experiences, and his resentment of the treatment he had received, as follows [1]:

'And his [Shakespeare's] sporting experiences
passed at times beyond orthodox limits. A
poaching adventure, according to a *credible* [2]
tradition, was the immediate cause of his long
severance from his native place. " He had,"
wrote Rowe in 1709, " by a misfortune common enough to young fellows, fallen into ill
company, and among them, some, that made
a frequent practice of deer-stealing, engaged

[1] Lee's *Shakespeare*, pp. 27–29.

[2] The italics in this and all the following quotations are my
own.

him with them more than once in robbing a
park that belonged to Sir Thomas Lucy of
Charlecote near Stratford. For this he was
prosecuted by that gentleman, *as he thought,
somewhat too severely ;* and, *in order to revenge*
that ill-usage, he made a ballad upon him, and
though this, probably the first essay of his
poetry, be lost, *yet it is said to have been so very
bitter* that it redoubled the prosecution against
him to that degree that he was obliged to leave
his business and family in Warwickshire and
shelter himself in London." The independent
testimony of Archdeacon Davies, who was
vicar of Saperton, Gloucestershire, late in the
seventeenth century, is to the effect that
Shakespeare " was much given to all unlucki-
ness in stealing venison and rabbits, particularly from Sir Thomas Lucy, who had him oft
whipt, and sometimes imprisoned, and at last
made him fly his native county to his great
advancement." The law of Shakespeare's day
(5 Eliz., cap. 21) punished deer-stealers with
three months' imprisonment and the payment
of thrice the amount of the damage done.

The tradition has been challenged on the
ground that the Charlecote deer-park was of
later date than the sixteenth century. But
Sir Thomas Lucy was an extensive game-
preserver, and owned at Charlecote a warren in

which a few harts or does doubtless found an
occasional home. Samuel Ireland was in-
formed in 1794 that Shakespeare stole the
deer, not from Charlecote, but from Fulbroke
Park, a few miles off, and Ireland supplied in
his *Views on the Warwickshire Avon*, 1795, an
engraving of an old farmhouse in the hamlet
of Fulbroke, where he asserted that Shakespeare was temporarily imprisoned after his
arrest. An adjoining hovel was locally known
for some years as Shakespeare's " deer-barn,"
but no portion of Fulbroke Park, which in-
cluded the site of these buildings (now removed), was Lucy's property in Elizabeth's
reign, and the amended legend, which was
solemnly confided to Sir Walter Scott in 1828
by the owner of Charlecote, seems pure invention.

The ballad which Shakespeare is reported to
have fastened on the park gates of Charlecote,
does not, as Rowe acknowledged, survive.
No authenticity can be allowed the worthless
lines beginning, " A parliament member, a
justice of peace," which were represented to
be Shakespeare's on the authority of an old
man who lived near Stratford and died in 1703.
But *such an incident as the tradition reveals
has left a distinct impress on Shakespearean
drama. Justice Shallow is beyond doubt a*

reminiscence of the owner of Charlecote.[1] According to Archdeacon Davies of Saperton,
Shakespeare's " *revenge* was so great " that he
caricatured Lucy as " Justice Clodpate," who
was (Davies adds) represented on the stage
as " a great man " and as bearing, in allusion
to Lucy's name, " three louses rampant for his
arms." Justice Shallow, Davies's " Justice
Clodpate," came to birth in the Second Part
of *Henry IV.* (1598), and he is represented in
the opening scene of the *Merry Wives of Windsor* as having come from Gloucestershire to
Windsor to make a Star-Chamber matter of
a poaching raid on his estate. The " three
luces hauriant argent " were the arms borne
by the Charlecote Lucys, and the dramatist's
prolonged reference in this scene to the
" dozen white luces " on Justice Shallow's
" old coat " fully establishes Shallow's identity
with Lucy.

The poaching episode is best assigned to
1585, but it may be questioned whether Shakespeare, on fleeing from Lucy's persecution, at
once sought an asylum in London.'

[1] As I have said elsewhere, I do not contend that Shakespeare did not have a part and a large part in the production of
the Shakespearean plays. My insistence is only that he was
not the transcendent genius to whom we owe their wonderful
and unrivalled poetry.

Halliwell gives the following traditions of Shakespeare's sharp encounters or exchanges of wit [1]:

Mr. Ben Jonson and Mr. Wm. Shakespeare being merry at a tavern, Mr. Jonson having begun this for his epitaph,—

> Here lies Ben Jonson, that was once one,

he gives it to Mr. Shakespeare to make up, who presently writes,

> Who while he lived was a slow thing
> And now being dead is nothing.

Another version is:

> Here lies Jonson,
> Who was one's son
> He had a little hair on his chin,
> His name was Benjamin !

an amusing allusion to his personal appearance, as any one may see who will turn to Ben's portrait.

Jonson.   If but stage actors all the world displays
Where shall we find spectators of their plays ?
Shakespeare.   Little or much of what we see we do;
We are all both actors and spectators too.

[1] Halliwell's *Shakespeare*, pp. 186, 187, 232, 241-245.

Ten in the hundred lies here ingrav'd;
'T is a hundred to ten his soul is not saved;
If any man ask, Who lies in this tomb ?
Oh! oh! quoth the devil, 't is my John-a-Combe.
Who lies in this tomb ?
Hough, quoth the devil, 't is my son, John-Combe.

The tradition is that the subject of the last six lines having died, Shakespeare then composed an epitaph as follows:

Howe'er he lived, judge not,
John Combe shall never be forgot,
While poor hath memory, for he did gather
To make the poor his issue; he their father,
As record of his tilth and seed,
Did crown him, in his latter need.

This is said to have been composed of a brother of John-a-Combe:

Thin in beard, and thick in purse,
Never man beloved worse,
He went to the grave with many a curse,
The devil and he had both one nurse.

A blacksmith is said to have accosted Shakespeare with,—

Now, Mr. Shakespeare, tell me, if you can,
The difference between a youth and a young man ?

To which the poet immediately replied,—

Thou son of fire, with thy face like a maple,
The same difference as between a scalded and a
  coddled apple.

An old tradition reports that being awakened
after a prolonged carouse, and asked to renew
the contest, he refused, saying, I have drunk
with

> Piping Pebworth, Dancing Marston,
> Haunted Hillborough, and Hungry Grafton
> With Dadging Exhall, Papist Wixford
> Beggarly Broom, and Drunken Bidford.

The lines inscribed on the slab above his
grave, preventing the removal of his bones,
according to the custom of that time, to the
adjacent charnel-house, are as follows:

> Good friend, for Jesus' sake forbeare
> To dig the dust enclosed heare;
> Bleste be the man that spare these stones,
> And curst be he that moves my bones.[1]

Mr. Lee gives a statement as to Shakespeare's propensity to litigation as follows[2]:

[1] Lee's *Shakespeare*, pp. 272, 273.
[2] Lee's *Shakespeare*, pp. 205, 206.

'As early as 1598 Abraham Sturley had suggested that Shakespeare should purchase the tithes of Stratford. Seven years later, on July 24, 1605, he bought for £440 of Ralph Huband an unexpired term of thirty-one years of a ninety-two years' lease of a moiety of the tithes of Stratford, Old Stratford, Bishopton, and Welcombe. The moiety was subject to a rent of £17 to the Corporation, who were the reversionary owners on the lease's expiration, and of £5 to John Barker, the heir of a former proprietor. The investment brought Shakespeare, under the most favorable circumstances, no more than an annuity of £38; and the refusal of persons who claimed an interest in the other moiety to acknowledge the full extent of their liability to the Corporation led that body to demand from the poet payments justly due from others. After 1609 he joined with two interested persons, Richard Lane of Awston, and Thomas Greene, the town clerk of Stratford, in a suit in Chancery to determine the exact responsibilities of all the tithe-owners, and in 1612 they presented a bill of complaint to Lord Chancellor Ellesmere, with what result is unknown. His acquisition of a part ownership in the tithes was fruitful in legal embarrassments.

Shakespeare inherited his father's love of liti-

gation, and stood rigorously by his rights in all his business relations. In March, 1600, he re-covered in London a debt of £7 from one John Clayton. In July, 1604, in the local court at Stratford, he sued one Philip Rogers, to whom he had supplied since the preceding March malt to the value of £1 19s. 10d., and had on June 25th lent 2s. in cash. Rogers paid back 6s., and Shakespeare sought the balance of the account, £1 15s. 10d. During 1608 and 1609 he was at law with another fellow-townsman, John Addenbroke. On February 15, 1609, Shakespeare, who was apparently represented by his solicitor and kinsman, Thomas Greene, obtained judgment from a jury against Addenbroke for the pay-ment of £6 and £1 5s. costs, but Addenbroke left the town, and the triumph proved barren. Shakespeare avenged himself by proceeding against one Thomas Horneby, who had acted as the absconding debtor's bail.'

The same author gives the following state-ment as to his reputation for *sportive ad-venture*[1]:

' Hamlet, Othello, and Lear were *rôles* in which he [Burbage] gained especial renown.

[1] Lee's *Shakespeare*, pp. 264–266.

But Burbage and Shakespeare were popularly credited with co-operation in less solemn enterprises. They were reputed to be companions in many *sportive* adventures. The sole anecdote of Shakespeare that is *positively known to have been recorded in his lifetime* relates that Burbage, when playing Richard III., agreed with a lady in the audience to visit her after the performance; Shakespeare, overhearing the conversation, anticipated the actor's visit and met Burbage on his arrival with the quip that " William the Conqueror was before Richard the Third."

Such gossip possibly deserves little more acceptance than the later story, in the same key, which credits Shakespeare with the paternity of Sir William D'Avenant. The latter was baptized at Oxford, on March 3, 1605, as the son of John D'Avenant, the landlord of the Crown Inn, where Shakespeare lodged in his journeys to and from Stratford. The story of Shakespeare's parental relation to D'Avenant was long current in Oxford, and was at times complacently accepted by the reputed son. Shakespeare is known to have been a welcome guest at John D'Avenant's house, and another son, Robert, boasted of the kindly notice which the poet took of him as a child. It is safer to adopt the less compromising version which

makes Shakespeare the godfather of the boy
William instead of his father. *But the antiquity
and persistence of the scandal belie the assumption that Shakespeare was known to his con-
temporaries as a man of scrupulous virtue.'*

All the extracts I have here quoted are from
writers who admit no question as to the authorship of the Shakespearean plays. And there
is nothing which they or any biography or
tradition bring to us which presents any act
or characteristic at all at variance with the
indications of these quotations. And it is
very remarkable how strong is the concurrence
of indications, from the slab above his grave,
from old, musty, and otherwise forgotten
records of court proceedings, and from traditions, whether from the hamlet of his birth or
the city where he wrought and succeeded.

I have not quoted the lines which have
been variously handed down as those which
the young Shakespeare affixed to the gate of
the wealthy and powerful Sir Thomas Lucy.
Their authenticity is doubtful.[1]   But that the

[1] The different versions of those lines are printed in the
appendix.

boy Shakespeare, weak and helpless for such a struggle, resented his treatment and answered back with the only weapon he had, risking and enduring being driven from his home and birthplace, and kept good the grudge in the days of his success, I think cannot be doubted. The records of court proceedings, the imprecation above his grave, both indicate a man of strong will and not unaccustomed to mastery. We may reject one or another of the retorts or sallies in verse, but we must, I think, agree, that the fact that they are brought to us by recorded and very old traditions, indicates a character or repute in accordance with their implication; and especially must this be so, when we find that they agree with the indications of other evidence not in any degree in question. These various indications support each other like the bundle of sticks which together could not be broken. From them I think we learn that Shakespeare, however pleasant or attractive at times, was not a man yielding or complacent to opposition or injury; but that he was a man of fighting blood or instincts, quick in wit and repartee, apt and

5

inclined for aggressive sally, ready to slash and lay about him in all encounters,—in short, a very Mercutio in temperament, and in the lively and constant challenges of his life.

I submit that the records we have of the life of William Shakespeare concur in indicating a man who could not have written the Sonnets under the circumstances and with the motives which they reveal.

It should not be overlooked that at the time these Sonnets were written, certainly as early as 1597 or 1598, Shakespeare was above pecuniary want, and had begun to make investments, and apparently regarded himself and was regarded as a wealthy man.[1]

[1] Lee's *Shakespeare*, pp. 193-196.

CHAPTER V

A S has been said before, the Sonnets obviously have a common theme. They
celebrate his friend, his beauty, his winning
and lovable qualities, leading the poet to forgive and to continue to love, even when his
friend has supplanted him in the favors of his
mistress. They are replete with compliment
and adulation. Little side views or perspec-
tives are introduced with a marvellous facility
of invention; and yet in them all, even in the
invocation to marry, in the jealousy of another
poet, in the railing to or of his false mistress,
is the face or thought of his friend, apparently
his patron. No other poet, it seems to me,
could have filled two thousand lines of poetry
with thoughts to, of, or relating to one person
of his own sex. Who that person was critics

73

have not agreed. But that he was a person who was somehow connected with the life-work of the poet seems beyond dispute.

Mr. Lee, speaking of the purpose of the Sonnets, at pages 125 and 126, says:

' Twenty Sonnets, which may for purposes of exposition be entitled " dedicatory " Sonnets, are addressed to one who is declared without periphrasis and without disguise to be a patron of the poet's verse (Nos. XXIII., XXVI., XXXII., XXXVII., XXXVIII., LXIX., LXXVII.-LXXXVI., C., CI., CIII., CVI.). In one of these,—Sonnet LXXVIII.,—Shakespeare asserted:

> So oft have I invoked thee for my Muse
> And found such fair assistance in my verse
> As every alien pen hath got my use
> And *under thee their poesy disperse.*

Subsequently he regretfully pointed out how his patron's readiness to accept the homage of other poets seemed to be thrusting him from the enviable place of pre-eminence in his patron's esteem.

Shakespeare's biographer is under an obligation to attempt an identification of the persons whose relations with the poet are defined so explicitly. The problem presented by the patron is simple. Shakespeare states unequivocally that he has no patron but one.

Sing [sc. O Muse!] to the ear that doth thy lays
    esteem,
And gives thy pen both skill and argument (C. 7–8).
For to no other pass my verses tend
Than of your *graces and your gifts to tell* (CIII.
    11–12).

The Earl of Southampton, the patron of his narrative poems, is the only patron of Shakespeare that is known to biographical research. No contemporary document or tradition gives the faintest suggestion that Shakespeare was the friend or dependent of any other man of rank.'

This quotation has been made because it is fair and accurate, because of the high authority of the book, but principally because it is the view of one who has no doubt that Shakespeare was the author of the Shakespearean plays. Research and ingenuity have been taxed to ascertain who was the unnamed and mysterious friend at whose feet are laid so many poetic wreaths, woven by such a master.

All discussion has assumed that this friend was a patron, who somehow greatly aided the poet, and to whom the poet felt himself greatly indebted. And so it was at once suggested that his friend was one of the nobility or peers of that age.

The Earl of Southampton (to whom by name *Venus and Adonis* and *Lucrece* were dedicated) has been very generally assumed to be the person intended. Lord Pembroke [William Herbert] has also been presented as the unnamed friend.

I think the Sonnets contain internal evidence that they were not addressed to either of these peers, AND WERE NOT ADDRESSED TO ANY ONE OF THEIR CLASS.

It is very remarkable how narrow is the range of these Sonnets,—how little they say, convey or indicate as to the person to whom they were addressed. From the first seventeen Sonnets we infer that the poet understood that his friend was unmarried; a line in Sonnet III. perhaps indicates a peculiar pride in his mother, and that it pleased him to be told that he resembled her; from a line in Sonnet XX., " A man in hue,'' etc., it has been inferred that his friend's beard or hair was auburn, and from Sonnets CXXXV. and CXXXVI. it has been inferred that his friend was familiarly called ''Will,'' or at any rate that his name was William. Obviously he was in some way a patron or helper to our poet, and to another poet as well [1]; he superseded the poet in the favors of his mistress; he was beautiful, attractive, genial, and sunny in disposition; that he was not infrequently responsive to lascivious love is indicated.[2] We have already fully considered what the Sonnets indicate as to his age. And now I put the inquiry: Is there anything else as to the poet's friend that these two thousand lines of poetry state or indicate? With diligent search I can find in all those lines no other fact indicated or stated as to this mysterious friend or patron.

In Sonnet CXXIV. the poet says:

If *my dear love were but* the child of state,
It might for Fortune's bastard be unfather'd.

---

[1] Sonnets LXXVIII., LXXIX., LXXX., LXXXV., LXXXVI.
[2] Sonnets XCV. and XCVI.

From that it has been argued that his friend was of the nobility, a " child of state."

Reading those two lines, or reading the entire Sonnet, it seems clear that if they contain any indication as to the station of his friend, the indication is rather against than in favor of his being of the nobility, " a child of state."

I do not think, however, that the lines allow any clear or certain deduction either way, but have called attention to them because they are often cited on this point.

In Sonnet XIII. occurs the line,

Who lets so fair a *house* fall to decay.

The word " house " as there used has been interpreted as though used in the sense of the House of York, and so made an implication that his friend was of a lordly line. Such a far-fetched and unusual interpretation should not be adopted unless clearly indicated. And the context clearly indicates that the phrase " so fair a house " is used as a metaphor for the poet's fair and beautiful body. If this inquiry were to be affected by far-drawn or even doubtful interpretations, I might quote from

Sonnet LXXXVI. There the poet, referring to his rival, says:

But when your *countenance* fill'd up his line.

By merely limiting the word *countenance* to its primary meaning, we may have the inference that his rival's verse was spoken or *acted* by his friend, and so that his friend was an actor. I do not think, however, that either of the two lines last cited are entitled to any weight as argument, but they illustrate the distinction between lines or Sonnets which may be the basis of surmise or conjecture, and those elsewhere cited, to which two different effects cannot be given without rending their words from their natural meaning.

The Earl of Southampton was born in 1573. He bore an historic name; fields, forests, and castles were his and had come to him from his ancestors; all of England that was most beautiful or most attractive was in the circle in which he moved and to which his presence contributed. In 1595 he appeared in the lists at a tournament in honor of the Queen; in 1596 and 1597 he joined in dangerous and successful naval and military expeditions; in 1598 he was married.[1] Is it conceivable that two thousand lines of adulatory poetry could have been written to and of him, and no hint appear of incidents like these? It is simply incredible. What is omitted rather than what is said clearly indicates that the life of the poet's friend presented no such incidents,— indeed no incidents which the poet chronicler of court and camp would interweave in his garlands of loving compliment.

Urging his friend to marry, the poet, comparing the harmony of music to a happy marriage, in Sonnet VIII. says:

Mark how one string, sweet husband to another,
Strikes each in each by mutual ordering;
Resembling sire and child and happy mother,
Who, all in one, one pleasing note do sing:
  Whose speechless song, being many, seeming one,
  Sings this to thee: "Thou single wilt prove none."

But is it not a little strange that the pen that drew Rosalind and Juliet should have gone no farther, when by a touch he could have filled it with suggestions of the fair, the

stately and the titled maidens who were in
the court life of that day, and whose names
and faces and reputed characters must have
been known to the poet, whatever his place or
station in London ? How would a tracing of a
mother, nobly born, or of a lordly but deceased
father, of some old castle, of some fair emi-
nence, of some grand forest, or of ancestral oaks
shading fair waters, have lightened the picture!
And could the poet who gave us the magnifi-
cent pictures of English kings and queens,
princes and lords—could that poet, writing to
and of one of the fairest of the courtly circle
of the reign of Elizabeth, so withhold his pen
that it gives no hint that his friend was in or
of that circle, or any suggestion of his most
happy and fortunate surroundings ? Surely,
in painting so fully the beauties of his friend,
the poet would have allowed to appear some
hint of the beauty of light and color in which
he moved.

I have before me in the book of Mr. Lee, a
copy of the picture of the Earl of Southampton
painted in Welbeck Abbey. The dress is of
the court; and the sword, the armor, the plume

and rich drapery all indicate a member of the
nobility. Could our great poet in so many
lines of extreme compliment and adulation
have always omitted any reference to the in-
signia of rank which were almost a part of the
young Earl; and would he always have escaped
all reference to coronet or sword, to lands or
halls, or to any of the employments or sports,
privileges or honors, then much more than now,
distinctive of a peer of the realm ?

And all that is here said equally repels the
inference that these Sonnets were addressed to
any person connected with the nobility. The
claim that they were addressed to Lord Pembroke [William Herbert] I think is exploded, if
it ever had substance.[1] Lord Pembroke did
not come to London until 1598 and was then
but eighteen years old. There is not a particle
of evidence that he and Shakespeare had any
relations or intimacy whatever.

While I regard the view that the Sonnets
were addressed to Southampton as entirely
untenable, it nevertheless has this basis, —
two of the Shakespearean poems were dedi-

[1] Lee's *Shakespeare*, p. 406.

cated to Southampton. At least we may say that, if they were addressed to any person of that class, there is a strong probability in his favor. And in order to consider that claim I would ask the reader to turn back to Sonnet II., page 23. That certainly is one of the very earliest of the Sonnets, almost certainly written when Shakespeare was not older than thirty and Southampton not over twenty-one years of age. With these facts in mind, the assumption that those lines were addressed to the Earl of Southampton becomes altogether improbable. Can we imagine a man of thirty, in the full glow of a vigorous and successful life, saying to a friend of twenty-one,—you should marry now, because when you are *forty years* old (about twice your present age and ten years above my own) your beauty will have faded and your blood be cold ?

We should not so slander the author of the Shakespearean plays.

The language of the Sonnets implies a familiarity and equality of intercourse not consistent with the theory that they were addressed

to a peer of England by a person in Shakespeare's position.'

The dedication of *Lucrece*, which apparently
was written in 1593, omits no reference to
title, and envinces no disposition or privilege
to ignore the rank or dignities of the Earl.   I
will quote no particular Sonnet on this point;
but the impression which the entire series seems
to me to convey, is that the poet was addressing a friend separated from him by no distinction of rank.   Sonnets XCVI. and XCVII.
are instances of such familiarity of address and
communication.

On the other hand, there is not a single indication which the Sonnets contain as to the
poet's friend which in any manner disagrees
with what we know of Shakespeare.   It may
be said that being married the invocation to
marry could not have been addressed to him.

---

¹ It was not until 1596 or 1599 that a coat of arms was
granted to John Shakespeare, the father of William.   That
appears to have been granted on the application of the son,
and to have been allowed, in part at least, because his wife,
the mother of William, was the daughter of Robert Arden,
gentleman.   The grant gave the father the title of Esquire
and not of Gentleman.   Lee's *Shakespeare*, pp. 187–190.

But the test is,—how did he pass, how was he
known in London, as married or unmarried ?
He is supposed to have come to London in
1586, or when he was twenty-two years of age,
and he was then married and had three chil-
dren.   He remained in London about twenty-
five years, and there is no indication that any
member of his family ever resided there or
visited him, and the clear consensus of opinion
seems to be that they did not.[1]   The indications that he had little love for his wife are
regrettably clear.[2]   When the earlier Sonnets
were written he must have been living there
about nine years, and must have had an income sufficient easily to have maintained his
family in the city.[3]   That he led a life noto-
riously free as to women cannot be questioned.
Traditions elsewhere referred to so indicate[4];
and whether the Sonnets were written by or to
him they equally so testify.   Under such cir-

[1] Lee's *Shakespeare*, p. 26 ; Halliwell's *Life of Shakespeare*,
p. 133 ; Grant White's *Introductory Life of Shakespeare*, pp.
25, 42.
[2] Lee's *Shakespeare*, pp. 22-26, 273, 274.
[3] Halliwell's *Shakespeare*, p. 172 , Lee's *Shakespeare*, pp.
193-196.
[4] See pp. 68-70, *supra*.

cumstances his friends or acquaintances would
not be led to presume that he was married,
but would assume the contrary. They would
have done or considered precisely as we do,
classing our friends as married or unmarried,
as their mode of life indicates. Hence the invocation to marry is entirely consistent with
the theory that the Sonnets were addressed to
Shakespeare. When Sonnet CIV. was written,
the poet had known his friend but three years [1];
the Sonnets referring to marriage are printed
first, and very probably were written much
earlier than Sonnet CIV., and perhaps when
their acquaintance was first formed. The fact
that the appeal ceases with the seventeenth
Sonnet, and that after that there is not even a
hint of marrying, or of female excellence and
beauty, perhaps indicates that the first seventeen Sonnets had provoked a disclosure which
restrained the poet from further reference to
those subjects.

The starting point in this chapter is the fact
stated by Mr. Lee, and I think conceded or as-

[1] The portion of Sonnet CIV. relevant to this point is
printed at page 26, *supra*.

sumed by all writers on these Sonnets,—that
they were written to some one intimately connected with the Shakespearean plays, either as
a patron or in some other manner. Many,
perhaps all, of the plays were produced, and in
that way published, at the theatre where Shakespeare acted. Those of the higher class or
order as well as those of the lower class were
published as his. Those most strenuous in
supporting the claims of authorship for Shakespeare, have, I think, generally conceded that
the plays, as we now have them, reveal in
various parts the work of more than one
author. And from that it has been suggested
that Shakespeare must have had a fellow-
worker,—a collaborator. Lee's *Shakespeare*,
Brandes's *Critical Study of Shakespeare*, and
the Temple edition of Shakespeare's works, are
practically agreed on this fact in relation to
Henry VI., *Henry VIII.*, *Titus Andronicus*,
and some other plays. There must have been
a very considerable degree of intercourse between the two persons who worked together
even on a single one of these plays. And
there are Sonnets which at least suggest a

degree and kind of intercourse and communication between the poet and his friend which
such a relation would require.

Chiding his friend for absence in Sonnets
LVII. and LVIII., the poet indicates such
waiting and watching as would come to him
had their relations been very intimate, and
perhaps indicates that he and his friend lodged
together.

Those Sonnets are as follows:

Being your slave, what should I do but tend
Upon the *hours* and times of your desire?
I have nó precious time at all to spend,
Nor *services* to do, *till you require.*
Nor dare I chide the *world-without-end hour*
Whilst I, my sovereign, *watch the clock for you,*
Nor think the bitterness of absence sour
When you have bid your servant once adieu;
Nor dare I question with my jealous thought
Where you may be, or your affairs suppose,
But, *like a sad slave, stay* and think of nought
Save, *where you are how happy* you make those.
   So true a fool is love that in your will,
   Though you do anything, he thinks no ill.

That God forbid that made me first your slave,
I should *in thought control your times of pleasure,*

Or at your hand the account of *hours* to crave,
Being your vassal, *bound to stay your leisure!*
O, let me suffer, being at your beck,
The imprison'd absence of your liberty;
And patience, tame to sufferance, bide each check,
Without accusing you of injury.
Be where you list, your charter is so strong
That *you yourself may privilege your time*
To what you will; to you it doth belong
Yourself to pardon of self-doing crime.
  I am to *wait*, though waiting so be hell,
  Not *blame your pleasure*, be it ill or well.

I am not unaware that there are other Sonnets which indicate that they lived apart,
though it is of course quite possible that they
lived apart at one time and together at another. But whether or not they at any time
lodged together, these Sonnets indicate that
their lives were brought together by some
common purpose, and that hours and seasons
of communication and perhaps of kindred
labor were frequent to them. Our affections
or friendships do not blossom in untilled
fields; it is the comradeship of common effort,
mutually helpful and beneficial, that more
than often determines the impalpable garments

and coverings of our lives. Certainly we may believe that the two characters that fill these two thousand lines of poetry did not live and move so far apart as were the busy actor at a theatre and the courted and adventurous peer of England.

If the friend to whom the Sonnets were addressed was Shakespeare, and if the author of the Sonnets and of the accredited Shakespearean plays was some " pale, wasted," and unknown student who sold his labors and his genius to another, we may perhaps see how they would have had frequent interviews and hours of labor, and how Shakespeare might have had all the relations to the poet, which the Sonnets imply of the poet's friend. But if Shakespeare, then well advanced both to fame and fortune, was the poet it is very difficult to imagine any one person who could have borne to him all the relations which the Sonnets indicate—patron or benefactor and familiar associate and companion; a rival and successor in the favors of his mistress, and a loved or at least cherished friend.

While I present the view that some unknown

student wrote, and Shakespeare adopted and
published, the Shakespearean plays, I do not
deny to Shakespeare a part, perhaps a large
part, in their production. As I have said,
there are many plays attributed to Shakespeare,
some or the greater portions of which are dis-
tinctively of a lower class than the greater plays
or the Sonnets. The theory of collaboration
affects at least six plays commonly classed as
Shakespearean, and perhaps others classed as
doubtful plays. Why is not the situation
satisfied if we ascribe to Shakespeare a capacity
equal to the composition of *Titus Andronicus?*
That is a play which seems to have been attractive from its plot and the character of its
incidents. In it, however, there are but few
lines that seem to be from the same author as
the Sonnets and the greater of the recognized
Shakespearean plays. The remainder of the
play has no poetic merit which raises it far
above the rustic poetry which is handed down
by tradition as Shakespeare's. And if we give
the unknown student all credit for authorship
of the finer poetry of the greater dramas, may
we not still assume that Shakespeare labored

with him, assisting in moulding into form adapted to the stage the poetry that burst from his friend with volcanic force; or that he perhaps sometimes suggested the side lights and sudden transitions which appear so often, —for instance, in the grave scene in *Hamlet* or the nurse's part in *Romeo and Juliet?* [1] And if some great unknown was the sole author and Shakespeare was the publisher and was to take part in the representation of these plays, may we not still, however they lodged, find ample occasion for the waiting hours of the poet, which would be entirely unexplained if the person addressed was the Earl of Southampton or some other member of the nobility ?

Such a view explains very much which is otherwise inexplicable. If into that series of publications came the genius of the unknown author of the Sonnets, touching some of the plays like stray sunbeams, and as the work

---

[1] These plays contain names of places and persons, and allusions and references, which could hardly have been made had Shakespeare been a stranger to their composition. In *As You Like It*, the forest has his mother's family name, " Arden " ; the allusion to Sir Thomas Lucy, has already been noticed. Page 63, *supra*.

progressed absorbing and filling all their framework,—it must yet be assumed that he did not
labor without recompense. And so we may
believe that Shakespeare from friend became
patron, and that this employment, coming as
the poet was passing to life's " steepy night,"
gave him the means and the leisure for those
dreams of lovers, of captains and of kings, so
visioned on his brain that he wrote of them
as of persons real and living. So regarding
the author of the Sonnets, we appreciate his
jealousy, when (as perhaps in *Henry VIII.*)
another and almost equal poet was employed,
and may understand how he could blame his
false mistress and yet forgive his friend. His
poetry and the opportunity and leisure for its
enjoyment was his real mistress, like the love
of Andromache for Hector displacing and
absorbing all other loves.

If the Sonnets were written by Shakespeare,
who the friend and patron so intimately related to the poet and his work was, is a riddle
still unsolved; but if they were written by
some unknown poet, the obvious and reason-

able inference is that they were addressed to Shakespeare.[1]

It may be asked why I would leave anything as the work of Shakespeare, if I deny to him the authorship of the greater plays. My answer is this: I believe he did not write the Sonnets; and if the Sonnets are the work of

---

[1] While I speak of the poet of the Sonnets and of the greater plays as unknown, I can but believe that the Sonnets, when carefully studied in connection with contemporaneous history and chronicles, will yet afford an adequate clew to his identification. It occurs to me that a promising line of inquiry might be made on this assumption,—that the poet was born about twenty years before Shakespeare and died soon after the production of the plays ceased, or when about sixty-five or seventy years of age ; that he had reverses and disappointments, perhaps humiliations ; that his name was William, and that he had written other works before he wrote the Shakespearean plays. It is also possible, although I think not probable, that the initials, W. H., appearing in the introduction to these Sonnets may refer to him. That he had produced earlier works, I think is shown by Sonnet LXXVI. The first lines of that Sonnet are as follows :

> " Why is my verse so barren of new pride,
> So far from variation of quick change?
> Why with the time do I not glance aside
> To new-found methods and to compounds strange?
> *Why write I still all one, ever the same,*
> *And keep inventions in a noted weed,*
> *That every word doth almost tell my name,*
> Showing their birth and where they did proceed?"

another, I think it fairly follows that the great dramas, considered as mere poetry, are so clearly in the same class as the Sonnets, that we must ascribe the authorship of the greater Shakespearean dramas to the same great unknown.

When it is once agreed that any considerable portions of the plays credited to Shakespeare are from different authors, almost the entire force of the argument resting on report or tradition is destroyed; because report or tradition is about equally satisfied and equally antagonized by ascribing to him the authorship of either section into which the admission of dual authorship concedes that they are divided.

That Shakespeare must have had a genius for dramatic work,—though not necessarily for poetry,—his success as a reputed dramatist and as a manager, all his history and traditions, very clearly indicate. And conceding him that, why is not the situation fully satisfied by considering that he was the lesser, or one of the lesser, rather than the greater of the collaborators; and that his knowledge of the stage and his talent for conceiving proper dramatic effects or situations, made his labors valuable to the greater poet, aiding him to give to his works a dramatic form and movement which many other great poets have entirely failed to attain. So considering, the Shakespearean plays will in some degree still seem to us the work of the gentle Shakespeare, although in large part the product of the older and more mature mind, the dreaming and loving recluse and student, who could say,—

Your name from hence immortal life shall have,
Though *I*, once gone, to all the world must die:
The earth can yield *me* but a common grave,
When *you* entombed in men's eyes shall lie.

And so believing, may we not still go with reverent feet to that grave upon the Avon? For there, as I conceive, sleeps he whose sunny graces won the undying love of the greatest of lovers and of poets, and whose assistance and support made possible the dreaming hours and days in which were delivered from his loving friend's overburdened brain the marvellous and matchless creations of the Shakespearean anthology.

CHAPTER VI

THE result of the preceding discussion, as it appears to me, is as follows:

The Sonnets were not written by Shakespeare, but it is very probable that he was the friend or patron around whom their poetry moves and to whom most of them are addressed.

Reading the entire series with that theory in mind, very many difficulties of interpretation are entirely overcome. Without this theory so many of the Sonnets seem blind, or obviously false or inaccurate, that many have been led to the inference of conceits, affectations, imitations, or hidden meanings. Adopting the theory here presented, there is neither reason nor excuse for giving to their words any other than their natural or ordinary meaning.

I would not deny to Shakespeare great talent. His success in and with theatres certainly forbids us to do so. That he had a bent or a talent for rhyming or for poetry, an early and persistent tradition and the inscription over his grave indicate. And otherwise there could hardly have been attributed to him so many plays beside those written by the author of the Sonnets.

Assuming that the Sonnets were not written by him, it would then seem clear that to Shakespeare, working as an actor, adapter or perhaps author, came a very great poet, one who outclassed all the writers of that day, in some respects all other writers; and that it is the poetry of that great unknown which, flowing into Shakespeare's work, comprises all, or nearly all of it which the world treasures or cares to remember. I would not dispute any claim made for Shakespeare for dramatic as distinguished from poetic talent, for wit, or comely or captivating graces. The case is all with him there,—at least there is no evidence to the contrary. But I insist that the Sonnets reveal another poet, and reveal that those great dramas, or at least that those portions of them which are in the same class or grade of poetry as the Sonnets, were the work of that great unknown.

APPENDIX

THE different versions of the verses which Shakespeare is alleged to have composed on Sir Thomas Lucy are as follows:

A parliamente member, a justice of peace,
At home a poore scare-crow, at London an asse;
If lowsie is Lucy, as some volke miscalle it,
Then Lucy is lowsie, whatever befalle it:
   He thinkes himselfe greate,
   Yet an asse in his state
We allowe by his eares but with asses to mate.
If Lucy is lowsie, as some volke miscalle it,
Sing lowsie Lucy, whatever befalle it.

    Sir Thomas was too covetous
      To covet so much deer,
    When horns enough upon his head
      Most plainly did appear.

    Had not his worship one deer left ?
      What then ?   He had a wife
    Took pains enough to find him horns
      Should last him during life.